Dr Rajan Thiagarajah gives short, life-changing insights about the blood of Jesus Christ, the Son of the Living God. His testimony of being a former Hindu and converting to Christianity motivates him even more to help Christians understand the power of the blood of Jesus Christ which enables us to overcome any work of the devil.

Sharon Daugherty
Senior Pastor
Victory Christian Center
Tulsa, Oklahoma

I was full of gratitude, wonder, and broken as I read the '31 Revelations about the Blood of Christ'. I will return to this book as a devotional reminder of the glorious, powerful truth of the shed blood of Jesus Christ.

Dr Wayde Goodall
President, Worldwide Family, Inc
Dean, Northwest University, College of Ministry, Kirkland, Washington

In this timely and important book, Dr. Rajan Thiagarajah has given us a revelation important to our time. We must never forget that Christianity is primarily a faith of covenant. The simplest definition of covenant is God saying, "if you give me what you have (your life), I'll give you what I have" (the completed work of Jesus Christ). What God grants to us has been procured by the blood of Christ. Dr. Rajan's book, *31 Revelations about the Blood of Christ*, is an amazing revelation of what the blood of Jesus has already appropriated for us as believers. This is the kind of revelation that could catapult you to God's abundant life. Read this book!!!

Ron McIntosh
Executive Director, Victory Bible Institute
Author of *The Greatest Secret, Quest for Revival,* and *Organic Christianity*

Dr. Rajan Thiagarajah effectively outlines the most important truths about the Blood of Jesus Christ in an easy to understand manner. This book will help you realize the power and magnitude of Christ's sacrifice on the cross and what it has purchased for you. It is a *must read* for every believer.

Dr. Edwin Miranda Jr.
Assistant Director, Victory Bible Institute, Tulsa, Oklahoma
Author of *Thriving in Life: Understanding the Power of Endurance, Discernment and the Favor of God* and *Passion for God*

For 2000 years the mighty blood of Jesus has never lost its power but sadly many Christians have never entered into a full revelation of that power. Dr Rajan Thiagarajah has produced a devotional aid that offers inspiration for 31 days of meditation on the blood of Christ. Each day's revelation has a key scripture text accompanied by supporting verses. As the reader delves further into the word and meditates on these key promises their faith in the precious blood of Jesus will be strengthened and renewed.

This book would be ideal for family devotionals, small group studies or even as a resource for churches doing a series on the blood of Christ. It is my pleasure to wholeheartedly recommend this resource and Dr Rajan himself to you. I have known him as a friend and anointed minister of the gospel for over a decade and have observed his ministry thrive as the mighty teaching and prophetic gift of God on his life has made way for him.

Phil Campbell
NSW State Chairman
Christian Outreach Centre, Australia

31
Revelations
about the
BLOOD
of CHRIST

WestBow Press books may be ordered through booksellers or by contacting:

WestBow Press
A Division of Thomas Nelson
1663 Liberty Drive
Bloomington, IN 47403
www.westbowpress.com
1-(866) 928-1240

Because of the dynamic nature of the Internet, any web addresses or links contained in this book may have changed since publication and may no longer be valid. The views expressed in this work are solely those of the author and do not necessarily reflect the views of the publisher, and the publisher hereby disclaims any responsibility for them.

Any people depicted in stock imagery provided by Thinkstock are models, and such images are being used for illustrative purposes only.

Unless otherwise indicated, all Scripture quotations are taken from The King James Version (KJV).

ISBN: 978-1-4497-1993-7 (e)
ISBN: 978-1-4497-1992-0 (sc)
ISBN: 978-1-4497-1995-1 (hc)

Library of Congress Control Number: 2011931404

Printed in the United States of America

WestBow Press rev. date: 6/16/2011

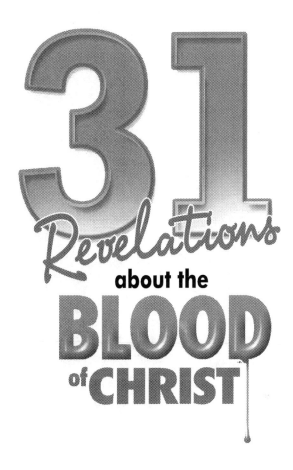

31 Revelations about the BLOOD of CHRIST

by

Dr Rajan Thiagarajah

WestBow
PRESS
A DIVISION OF THOMAS NELSON

CONTENTS

Introduction

One day whilst I was in prayer, I had the Bible opened and was meditating upon the word and praying the scriptures. One of the scriptures caught my attention.

Romans 3:25

> *"Whom God hath set forth to be a propitiation through faith in His blood, to declare His righteousness for the remission of sins that are past through the forbearance of God".*

The words "faith in His blood" began to speak to me. At that very moment the Holy Spirit impressed in my spirit the need to have faith in His blood.

Faith only comes through one way, which is the word of God.

Romans 10:17

> *"So then faith cometh by hearing and hearing by the word of God".*

Therefore, in order for us to walk in faith in His blood, we need to continually hear from the word what the blood of Jesus has done for us.

This is the reason why the Spirit of God inspired me to write about the 31 revelations of the blood.

As you read it every day, it will build faith in your heart and you will know the power of the blood of Jesus.

Revelation no. 1

The Blood
of Jesus Christ
Made the Way

The Word of God is comprised of covenants.

God's dealings with man have always been through covenants.

God Almighty has given us a covenant to show forth His utmost commitment to us through the terms of the covenant.

Covenant gives a child of God the assurance of His steadfastness to us.

Psalm 89:28

> *"My mercy will I keep for him for evermore and my covenant shall stand fast with him."*

Psalm 89:34

> *"My covenant will I not break, nor alter the thing that is gone out of my lips."*

A covenant is a strong agreement
or a contract between two parties
which needs to be ratified.

The way God's covenants were ratified was through the shedding of the blood.

1. Abram in Genesis 15:7-18 entered into a covenant through the shedding of blood.

2. Abram in Genesis 17:9-11 establishes a covenant through the shedding of the blood.

Almighty God declares in:

Psalm 50:5

> **"Gather my saints together unto me:**
> **those that have made a covenant**
> **with me by sacrifice."**

Today we have a better covenant based upon better promises.

Hebrews 8:6
> **"But now hath he obtained a more excellent**
> **ministry by how much also he is the mediator**
> **of a better covenant, which was established**
> **upon better promises."**

One of the reasons that
we have a better covenant
is because the New Covenant
was ratified by
the blood of God's Son.

This is clearly explained in:

Hebrews 9:12 "Neither by the blood of goats and calves, but by his own blood he entered in once into the holy place, having obtained eternal redemption for us."

In the Old Covenant when Aaron entered into the Holy of Holies, he entered with the blood of substitute, being the blood of the animals. There was forgiveness, not cleansing from sin. God looked away, in other words He turned His face away.

Under the New Covenant,
when the Son of God Jesus Christ
entered into the holy place,
the sin was not just covered,
it was put away. He entered with
His own blood as man Christ.
That is why He
guarantees the New Covenant.

Hebrews 7:22

> **"By so much was Jesus made a surety of a
> better testament."**

As we journey through this book I want you to understand the living eternal power of the blood of Jesus Christ.

Romans 10:17 says,

> **"So then faith cometh by hearing and hearing
> by the Word of God."**

As you learn about the blood, I pray that you will begin to grow in faith in His blood.

Romans 3:25

> **"Whom God hath set forth to be a
> propitiation through faith in his blood,
> to declare his righteousness
> for the remission of sins that are past, through
> the forbearance of God."**

Hebrews 7:22

**"By so much was
Jesus made a surety of
a better testament."**

Revelation no. 2

The Blood of Jesus Christ Cleanses Us

1 John 1:7

**"But if we walk in the light, as he is in the
light, we have fellowship one with another,
and the blood of Jesus Christ his Son cleanseth
us from all sin."**

The word 'cleansing' means to make clean, to purify, to
remove any physical stains and dirt.

The Word of God states that the blood of Jesus Christ
has the power to make us clean, to purify us and to
remove any physical stain or dirt that we have through
sin.

1 John 1:7 states the blood cleanseth. That means it
is in the present tense. I am sure you will be glad and
joyful to know that the blood of Jesus Christ which was
shed for you two thousand years ago is cleansing you
right now.

In order for the blood of Jesus to cleanse us, 1 John 1:7
gives us certain conditions.

1. We must walk in the light

2. We must have fellowship
   with one another

The Word clearly states that the blood cleanses us from all sin. The words 'all sin' are important. We must be conscious that the blood of Jesus cleanses us from all sin. When we have a consciousness of the blood of Jesus, it removes from us the consciousness of guilt.

Let us declare:

"The blood of Jesus Christ, the Son of living God cleanseth me from all sin."

Amen

1 John 1:7

"*But if we walk in the light,
as he is in the light,
we have fellowship one
with another, and the blood
of Jesus Christ his Son
cleanseth us from all sin.*"

Revelation no. 3

The Blood
of Jesus Christ
Provides Us Forgiveness

Ephesians 1:7

"In whom we have redemption through his blood, the forgiveness of sins, according to the riches of his grace"

The blood of Jesus provides us forgiveness for our offences, shortcomings and trespasses.

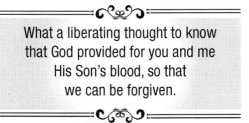

What a liberating thought to know that God provided for you and me His Son's blood, so that we can be forgiven.

In the Old Covenant they had to use the blood of animals to cover their sin and to be forgiven – not on a permanent basis. The offering was a substitute and the effect of the offering was temporary.

The Word of God clearly states in:

1 John 1: 9

"If we confess our sins, he is faithful and just to forgive us our sins, and to cleanse us from all unrighteousness."

Now, we have a better covenant through the blood of Jesus. The New Covenant provides us with forgiveness.

A forgiven heart carries no guilt
and has the ability and the divine
power to forgive others.

Let us declare:

"The blood of Jesus Christ has forgiven me."

Amen

1 John 1: 9

"If we confess our sins,
he is faithful and just
to forgive us our sins,
and to cleanse us from all
unrighteousness."

Revelation no. 4

The Blood
of Jesus Christ
has Redeemed Us

Ephesians 1:7

> **"In whom we have redemption through his blood, the forgiveness of sins, according to the riches of his grace."**

Redemption is a legal word. It means a price has been paid to buy back a property.

The blood of Jesus paid the price for us to be redeemed.

Leviticus 17:11

> **"For the life of the flesh is in the blood: and I have given it to you upon the altar to make an atonement for your souls: for it is the blood that maketh an atonement for the soul."**

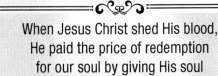

When Jesus Christ shed His blood, He paid the price of redemption for our soul by giving His soul as a ransom.

Because of the blood of Jesus, you have been purchased by God to enjoy life.

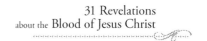
Jesus Christ, the Son of the living God said in:

John 10:10

> **"The thief cometh not, but for to steal,
> and to kill, and to destroy: I am come that
> they might have life, and that they might have
> it more abundantly."**

Let us declare:

"The blood of Jesus Christ has redeemed me."

Amen

Ephesians 1:7

**"In whom we have redemption
through his blood,
the forgiveness of sins, according
to the riches of his grace."**

Revelation no. 5

**The Blood
of Jesus Christ
has Translated Us
Into the
Kingdom of God**

Colossians 1:13-14

**"Who hath delivered us from the power
of darkness, and hath translated us into
the kingdom of his dear Son:
14 In whom we have redemption through
his blood, even the forgiveness of sins."**

The power of the blood took us out of darkness. Before we were redeemed by the blood we were under the dominion of the devil. His Kingdom is the Kingdom of darkness.

The power and the price of the blood
of Jesus translated us from the
dominion and the power of the devil
to the Kingdom of Light
(Kingdom of God).

I want you to see that the blood of Jesus has changed your position.

Now you stand in a Kingdom ruled and reigned by God's Son, Jesus Christ.

In the kingdom of God there is no calamity, no bondage, no sickness; freedom and liberty is the way of life.

So God, through the blood of His Son
has translated you from:

1. Bondage to freedom
2. Calamity to peace
3. Sickness and disease to health
4. Death to life
5. Tragedy to safety
6. Lack to abundance
7. Curse to the blessing of Abraham
8. Sorrow to joy and peace

Let us declare:

"The blood of Jesus Christ has translated me from the power of darkness to the Kingdom of His dear Son, Jesus."

Amen

Colossians 1:13-14

---

*"Who hath delivered us
from the power of darkness,
and hath translated us into
the kingdom of his dear Son:
14 In whom we have redemption
through his blood,
even the forgiveness of sins."*

---·୧୬ୠ୬ଚ··---

Revelation no. 6

--··୧ ୬ ଚ··--

The Blood
of Jesus Christ
Justifies Us

Romans 5:9

> **"Much more then, being now justified
> by his blood, we shall be saved
> from wrath through him."**

The word 'justified' means just as. The Word of God is saying to us, because of the blood of Jesus we are justified; just as if we have never sinned.

It is only the blood of Jesus that can justify an individual. The Word clearly states that we all have sinned.

Romans 3:23

> **"For all have sinned, and come short
> of the glory of God."**

Therefore we need to be justified by the blood of Jesus to be in right standing with God.

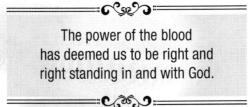

The power of the blood
has deemed us to be right and
right standing in and with God.

Justification through the blood of Jesus sets us free from works. We are not justified by our own works; we are justified because of the shed blood of Jesus.

The truth of justification through
the blood of Jesus must continually
be in our thoughts and
consciousness. This will set us free
from negative thoughts that the
enemy tries to bring upon us.

Let us declare:

"The blood of Jesus Christ has justified me, just as if
I have never sinned."

Amen

Romans 5:9

"*Much more then,
being now justified by his blood,
we shall be saved from wrath
through him.*"

Revelation no. 7

The Blood
of Jesus Christ
has Reconciled Us

Colossians 1:20

> **"And, having made peace through the blood of his cross, by him to reconcile all things unto himself; by him, I say, whether they be things in earth, or things in heaven."**

The word 'reconcile' means to change from one condition to another, so as to remove all enmity and leave no impediment to unity and peace.

The blood of Jesus Christ has removed all enmity between God and man, so that we can be reconciled to Him.

Reconciliation restores our position with God and in God.

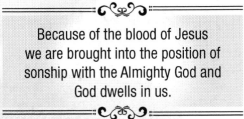

Because of the blood of Jesus we are brought into the position of sonship with the Almighty God and God dwells in us.

When we are reconciled to God through the blood of Jesus Christ, our hearts become filled with God's unconditional love, so that we can reach out to others, having a ministry of reconciliation.

Let us declare:

"The blood of Jesus Christ has reconciled me."

Amen

Colossians 1:20

---

*"And, having made peace
through the blood of his cross,
by him to reconcile all things
unto himself; by him, I say,
whether they be things in earth,
or things in heaven."*

The Blood
of Jesus Christ
has Given Us
Peace with God

Colossians 1:20

> **"And, having made peace through the blood of his cross, by him to reconcile all things unto himself; by him, I say, whether they be things in earth, or things in heaven."**

I want you to think of the phrase "Peace with God".

When God created man, He created him to have fellowship with Him. As the Word of God says, God was looking for Adam in the cool of the day.

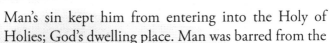

When man sinned and disobeyed God, he lost his union and communion with God. There became a separation between God and man because God is holy.

Man's sin kept him from entering into the Holy of Holies; God's dwelling place. Man was barred from the Holy of Holies by the Ten Commandments.

True peace can only reign in our hearts when we have made peace with our Master. That is why we see so many individuals who have fame, money and position but they have no peace. Why? They have not accepted the Prince of Peace who shed His blood to give them peace with God.

We have peace with God because we have faith in the shed blood of Jesus and we received the Prince of Peace, our Lord and Saviour.

Let us declare:

"Jesus Christ has made peace with God for me and my household through His blood in Jesus Name."

"The blood of Jesus Christ has given me and my household peace with God."

Amen

Ephesians 2:14

"*For he is our peace,
who hath made both one,
and hath broken down
the middle wall of partition
between us.*"

Revelation no. 9

The Blood
of Jesus Christ
has Given Us
Access to the
Throne of God

Hebrews 10:19

"Having therefore, brethren, boldness to enter into the holiest by the blood of Jesus."

In the Old Covenant we see that the Holy of Holies was not accessible to anyone apart from the High Priest who entered once a year.

The High Priest had to comply to strict rules and regulations that needed to be fulfilled in order to enter the Holy of Holies where God's presence dwelt.

Failing to comply with the Law would result in the death of the High Priest. This gives us a clear picture of the holiness of God and also the fact that sin separates us from God's presence.

When Jesus Christ shed His blood
and became the perfect sacrifice
on the cross for our sin, the way was
open to access God's throne
through His blood.

I want you to remember the word 'boldness' in Hebrews 10:19.

> We do not have to worship God
> from afar anymore. We can enter
> into the Holy of Holies through
> the blood of His Son.

That is why the Word of God states in:

Ephesians 2:19

> **"Now therefore ye are no more strangers and
> foreigners, but fellowcitizens with the saints,
> and of the household of God."**

The blood of Jesus Christ has brought us from the outer court into the inner court.

Let us declare:

"The blood of Jesus has given me access to the throne of God at any time and in any place in Jesus Name."

Amen

Hebrews 10:19

"*Having therefore, brethren, boldness to enter into the holiest by the blood of Jesus.*"

The Blood of Jesus Christ has the Power to Purge Our Conscience

Hebrews 9:14

**"How much more shall the blood of Christ,
who through the eternal Spirit offered himself
without spot to God,
purge your conscience from dead works
to serve the living God?"**

In our memory bank we have two sets of data. One which is lodged in our conscience and the other in our sub-conscience.

The memory data that is in our conscience, we are able to access at our own will and at anytime.

The memory data that is in our subconscious we are not able to access at will. It is only accessible by an event or situation which triggers the memory in the subconscious. For example, when you hear a certain song, you immediately remember the place where you were when you first heard it and also the events that occurred during that time.

Some memories that are in our sub-conscious are good and some are bad. Many individuals fall into fear, anger and temptation through ungodly memories that are lodged in their sub-conscious.

The only element that washes all the dead and unproductive memories in our conscience is the blood of Jesus.

> When our conscience is clear,
> we will begin to see God's purpose
> and His will for our lives clearly.
> That is why the Word states the blood
> can purge our conscience from
> dead works to serve the living God.

Let us declare:

"I apply the cleansing power of the blood of Jesus to my mind, memory cells, conscious and subconscious to purge all dead works to serve the living God."

Amen

Hebrews 9:14

*"How much more shall
the blood of Christ, who through the
eternal Spirit offered himself without
spot to God, purge your conscience
from dead works
to serve the living God?"*

The Blood of Jesus Christ Has Made Us Nigh

Ephesians 2:13

**"But now in Christ Jesus ye who
sometimes were far off are made nigh
by the blood of Christ."**

We were far away and alienated from the presence of God. When you are far away from God you are not able to enjoy the goodness of God.

Sin separated us from God. There was a separation between man and God.

Ephesians 2:14

**"For he is our peace, who hath made
both one, and hath broken down the
middle wall of partition between us."**

Through the sacrifice on the cross,
Jesus Christ has destroyed
the separation whereby we can enjoy
the presence of God.

Sin also brought enmity against God. Once again His sacrifice has abolished the enmity and translated us nigh to God.

That is why Ephesians 2:19 states:

"Now therefore ye are no more strangers and foreigners, but fellowcitizens with the saints, and of the household of God."

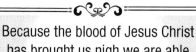

Because the blood of Jesus Christ has brought us nigh we are able to enjoy the legal right of being the household of God.

Let us declare:

"The blood of Jesus has brought me nigh and made me the household of God."

Amen

Ephesians 2:13

*"But now in Christ Jesus
ye who sometimes
were far off are made nigh by
the blood of Christ."*

Revelation no. 12

---

*The Blood
of Jesus Christ
Made it Possible
For Us to Commune
in the Blood*

1 Corinthians 10:16

> *"The cup of blessing which we bless,*
> *is it not the communion of the blood*
> *of Christ? The bread which we break,*
> *is it not the communion of the body*
> *of Christ"*

Remember, when we take communion in accordance with:

1 Corinthians 11:23-25

> *"For I have received of the Lord that which*
> *also I delivered unto you, That the Lord Jesus*
> *the same night in which he was betrayed took*
> *bread:*
>
> *24 And when he had given thanks, he brake*
> *it, and said, Take, eat: this is my body, which*
> *is broken for you: this do in remembrance of*
> *me." 25 In the same way, after supper he took*
> *the cup, saying, "This cup is the new covenant*
> *in my blood; do this, whenever you drink it, in*
> *remembrance of me."*

We are in commune with the blood of our Lord Jesus Christ.

This union and communion is deeper and is of a life giving nature whereby our hearts are knit together with the heart of God.

> There is no closer union and
> communion with the Lord than
> the commune in the blood.

That is why we read in the book of Acts chapter 2:42 onwards, that as the apostles broke bread from house to house and celebrated the union with God, He began to bless them.

The blood of Christ knits our hearts with the heart of God.

Let us declare:

"I have communion in the blood of God's Son; therefore my heart is knit with the heart of God."

Amen

1 Corinthians 10:16

"*The cup of blessing which we bless, is it not the communion of the blood of Christ? The bread which we break, is it not the communion of the body of Christ?*"

---- ᕤᕫ᠍ᕫ᠍ᕤ ----

Revelation no. 13

---- ᕤᕫ᠍ᕫ᠍ᕤ ----

*The Blood
of Jesus Christ
Connects and
Keeps Us
in the Covenant*

Hebrews 13:20

"Now the God of peace, that brought again from the dead our Lord Jesus, that great shepherd of the sheep, through the blood of the everlasting covenant."

A covenant is a strong binding agreement. The Word of God contains two covenants; the Old Covenant and the New Covenant.

All covenants require four
basic elements:

1. It is binding
2. It is holy
3. It must be ratified
4. If a covenant is broken
   there is a penalty

The New Covenant, the better covenant was ratified by the blood of Jesus Christ.

Hebrews 9:12

"Neither by the blood of goats and calves, but by his own blood he entered in once into the holy place, having obtained eternal redemption for us."

Hebrews 8:6

"But now hath he obtained a more excellent ministry, by how much also he is the mediator of a better covenant, which was established upon better promises."

The blood of Jesus brought us into an everlasting, better covenant. The blood keeps us in that covenant.

Every time we declare
the blood of Jesus Christ,
the blood reminds God Almighty
of the covenant we have with Him
through His Son.

Remember, all of God's blessings
can only be appropriated
through the covenant.

Let us declare:

"The blood of Jesus Christ has brought me into an everlasting better covenant and it keeps me in that covenant."

Amen

Hebrews 13:20

"*Now the God of peace,*
that brought again
from the dead our Lord Jesus,
that great shepherd of the sheep,
through the blood of
the everlasting covenant."

Revelation no. **14**

The Blood of Jesus Christ Has Made Us Priests and Kings

Revelation 1:5-6

> *"And from Jesus Christ, who is the faithful*
> *witness, and the first begotten of the dead,*
> *and the prince of the kings of the earth.*
> *Unto him that loved us, and washed us from*
> *our sins in his own blood, 6 And hath made us*
> *kings and priests unto God and his Father; to*
> *him be glory and dominion forever and ever.*
> *Amen."*

The blood of Jesus Christ
has taken us out of the pit
and has elevated us to be
kings and priests unto God.

In the book of Hebrews the Word says that He is able to save us to the uttermost. I once heard someone say that the Lord had lifted him from the guttermost to the uttermost.

The blood of Jesus has the power to lift us up.

Hebrews 8:25

> *"Wherefore he is able also to save them*
> *to the uttermost that come unto God*
> *by him, seeing he ever liveth to make*
> *intercession for them."*

> As a priest we are to worship,
> honour and serve God.
> As a king we rule righteously.
>
> The blood of Jesus Christ
> has given us a position in life.

Remember, it does not matter what your earthly position is, the blood of Jesus has obtained for you and me a heavenly position which is eternal.

Jesus our Lord washed our sins with His own blood to make us kings and priests unto His Father.

What a glorious redeemer our Lord is.

Let us declare:

"Thank you Lord that through Your blood You have made me a king and a priest unto Your Father and my God."

Amen

Revelation 1:5-6

"And from Jesus Christ,
who is the faithful witness,
and the first begotten of the dead,
and the prince of the kings
of the earth. Unto him that
loved us, and washed us
from our sins in his own blood,
6 And hath made us kings and
priests unto God and his Father;
to him be glory and dominion
forever and ever. Amen."

Revelation no. **15**

The Blood
of Jesus Christ
Gives Us the
Power to Overcome

Revelation 12:11

> **"And they overcame him by the blood
> of the Lamb, and by the word
> of their testimony; and they loved
> not their lives unto the death."**

The above verse clearly states that the blood of Jesus is one of the elements that is needed to overcome the devil.

Let me state the above scripture in a manner that we will all be able to remember and apply.

"I overcome Satan by personally testifying what the Word says the blood of Jesus does for me."

When we declare what the Word
of God says the blood of
Jesus does for us, it gives us faith
and power to overcome.

Remember, we are overcomers
through His Word and His blood.

So God has placed in our hands
a divine weapon, a weapon that
has the power to destroy
the work of the devil and
give us the ability to overcome.
The divine weapon is
the blood of Jesus.

2 Corinthians 10:4

**"For the weapons of our warfare are not
carnal, but mighty through God to the pulling
down of strong holds."**

Let us declare:

"I overcome Satan by declaring what the Word says
the blood of Jesus does for me."

I have been redeemed by the blood from sickness,
disease and plagues into divine health.

Colossians 1:13-14

"Who hath delivered us from the power of darkness, and hath translated us into the kingdom of his dear Son. 14 In whom we have redemption through his blood, even the forgiveness of sins:"

I thank You that the blood of Jesus speaks mercy and grace for me and my household.

Hebrews 12:24

"And to Jesus the mediator of the new covenant, and to the blood of sprinkling, that speaketh better things than that of Abel."

Amen

Above are some of the examples of how you can declare the blood. As you take hold of all the revelations of the blood of Jesus in the Word of God and begin to declare them, faith and power will be born in your life to overcome.

Revelation no. 16

The Blood
of Jesus Christ
Has Given Us
Eternal Life

John 6:53-54

> **"Then Jesus said unto them,**
> **Verily, verily, I say unto you,**
> **Except ye eat the flesh of the Son of man, and**
> **drink his blood, ye have no life in you. 54**
> **Whoso eateth my flesh,**
> **and drinketh my blood, hath eternal life; and**
> **I will raise him up at the last day."**

The blood of Jesus has given us eternal life. Many Christians do not have the concept that they have eternal life.

1 John 5:13

> **"These things have I written unto you that**
> **believe on the name of the Son of God;**
> **that ye may know that ye have eternal life,**
> **and that ye may believe on the name**
> **of the Son of God."**

The above scripture clearly states that we have eternal life. What is eternal life?

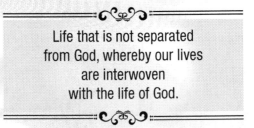

Life that is not separated
from God, whereby our lives
are interwoven
with the life of God.

The blood of Jesus has brought eternity into our lives. We will spend eternity in God's presence.

1 John 5:11

> **"And this is the record, that God hath given to us eternal life, and this life is in his Son."**

The blood of Jesus has made it possible for us to have and enjoy the life of the Son of God.

Remember, God is not eternal but eternity dwells in Him. Through the blood of Jesus we become partakers of that eternal life of God.

Let us declare:

"Through the blood of Jesus I have eternal life."

Amen

John 6:53-54

*"Then Jesus said unto them,
Verily, verily, I say unto you,
Except ye eat the flesh of the Son
of man, and drink his blood,
ye have no life in you.
54 Whoso eateth my flesh,
and drinketh my blood,
hath eternal life; and I will
raise him up at the last day."*

---·ᏜᏙᏜᏙ·---
Revelation no. 17
---·ᏜᏙᏜᏙ·---

The Blood of Jesus Christ Has Broken Enmity between God and Man

Ephesians 2:13-16

> **"But now in Christ Jesus ye who sometimes
> were far off are made nigh by the blood
> of Christ. 14 For he is our peace, who hath
> made both one, and hath broken down the
> middle wall of partition between us
> 15 Having abolished in his flesh the enmity,
> even the law of commandments contained
> in ordinances; for to make in himself of twain
> one new man, so making peace;
> 16 And that he might reconcile both unto
> God in one body by the cross, having slain the
> enmity thereby."**

God created Adam to have fellowship with Him. That is why the Word says that God would come to see His prized creation Adam in the cool of the day to have communion with Him.

When Adam disobeyed God, he substituted God's will with his will. That was the beginning of sin and rebelliousness.

Sin and rebelliousness separates
humanity from God and His love.
The sinful nature and the
rebelliousness nature are natures
that do not allow God's will
to reign in a life.

Jesus Christ the Son of the Living God has come to fulfil the Law. Why did He fulfil the Law? God had to introduce the Law to make humanity realize that they were of a sinful, rebellious nature and the consequences of it were enmity between man and God. Man was not capable of keeping the Law and in the Old Covenant they had to offer sacrifices every year to atone for their sin.

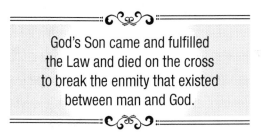

God's Son came and fulfilled
the Law and died on the cross
to break the enmity that existed
between man and God.

That is why today you can call God your heavenly Father.

Let us declare:

"The blood of Jesus Christ has broken the enmity between me and God. The blood of Jesus has established a living relationship between me and God."

Amen

Ephesians 2:15

"Having abolished in his flesh the enmity, even the law of commandments contained in ordinances; for to make in himself of twain one new man, so making peace"

The Blood
of Jesus Christ
Sanctifies Us

Hebrews 13:12

> *"Wherefore Jesus also, that he might sanctify the people with his own blood, suffered without the gate."*

The word 'sanctify' means to make one holy but it also means to separate.

The blood of Jesus not only made us holy by washing away our sins but it separated us to worship, honour and serve God.

The blood of Christ has sanctified us for God's purpose.

In the Old Covenant the altar and the offering had to be sanctified.

Exodus 29:37

> *"Seven days thou shalt make an atonement for the altar, and sanctify it; and it shall be an altar most holy: whatsoever toucheth the altar shall be holy."*

We see in the above scripture that the altar had to be sanctified by blood for it to be holy for God's purpose.

In the New Covenant we see the cross of Calvary as the ultimate altar where God's Son was sacrificed. The blood of the Son of God not only sanctified the altar but also everyone who will accept and receive the perfect sacrifice on the cross.

The altar was sanctified by the blood of Jesus and the offering is sanctified by the altar.

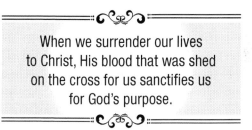

When we surrender our lives to Christ, His blood that was shed on the cross for us sanctifies us for God's purpose.

Let us declare:

"The blood of Jesus Christ has sanctified me and set me apart to honour, worship and serve the living God."

Amen

Hebrews 13:12

---

*"Wherefore Jesus also,
that he might sanctify the people
with his own blood, suffered
without the gate."*

Revelation no. 19

The Blood
of Jesus Christ
Makes Us Perfect
in the Sight of God

Hebrews 10:14

"For by one offering he hath perfected for ever them that are sanctified."

We learn that the blood of Jesus has sanctified us. Sanctification by the blood makes one holy.

The Apostle Peter states
in the Word: 1 Peter 1:16
"Because it is written.
Be ye holy for I am holy."

What makes us holy is not our righteousness but the righteousness of our Lord Jesus. He gave us His righteousness by shedding His very blood on the cross of Calvary.

When we are clothed in His righteousness and covered by His blood it elevates our position from the natural to the supernatural.

When God the Father looks upon us He sees our new found position in Christ which is perfect because of the blood of Jesus. That is why the Word of God declares:

1 Peter 2:9

> **"But ye are a chosen generation, a royal
> priesthood, an holy nation, a peculiar people;
> that ye should shew forth the praises
> of him who hath called you out of darkness
> into his marvellous light:"**

Let us declare:

"The blood of Jesus has not only sanctified me, it has also made me perfect in the sight of God."

Amen

Hebrews 10:14

"**For by one offering he hath perfected for ever them that are sanctified.**"

Revelation no. 20

The Blood
of Jesus Christ
Brings the Manifestation
of the Holy Spirit

1 John 5:7-8

> **"For there are three that bear record in heaven, the Father, the Word, and the Holy Ghost: and these three are one.**
> **8 And there are three that bear witness in earth, the Spirit, and the water, and the blood: and these three agree in one."**

As God the Father, Son, the Word and the Holy Ghost bear record in heaven, similarly the Spirit, the blood and the water being the Word of God, agrees on earth.

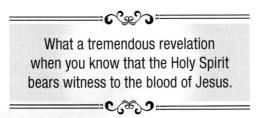

What a tremendous revelation when you know that the Holy Spirit bears witness to the blood of Jesus.

The blood that our Master shed is not ordinary blood. This is unique, heavenly blood full of power and life. It is the Holy Spirit that bears witness to our spirit about the divine work of the blood of Jesus.

In order for the Spirit of God to bear witness to the blood of Jesus, the blood must be appropriated and declared.

The moment we declare what the
Word says the blood of Jesus
does for us, the Holy Ghost
comes with the power
of heaven to demonstrate
and to manifest that truth.

The spirit manifests His full power and works effectively among us only through the blood. What a glorious blood that summons the Spirit of God to be present.

Let us declare:

"As I declare the blood of Jesus and its attributes upon me, my household, my situation and circumstances, the blessed Holy Spirit comes to manifest the resurrection power."

Amen

1 John 5:7-8

*"For there are three that
bear record in heaven, the Father,
the Word, and the Holy Ghost:
and these three are one.
8 And there are three that bear
witness in earth, the Spirit,
and the water, and the blood:
and these three agree in one."*

Revelation no. 21

The Blood of Jesus Christ has Given Us the Indwelling Spirit

Hebrews 9:12

"Neither by the blood of goats and calves, but by his own blood he entered in once into the holy place, having obtained eternal redemption for us."

The reason for eternal redemption is that man can become a habitation of heaven.

What a great salvation our Lord has provided for us. Man born in sin, shaped in iniquity, forgiven, cleansed, purified outside and inside by the precious blood of Jesus to be made a habitation of God.

Paul, the Apostle reminds us in:
1 Corinthians 3:16

*"Know ye not that ye
are the temple of God,
and that the Spirit of God
dwelleth in you?"*

The purpose of the blood of Jesus is
to make us the habitation of God.

The outpouring of the blood was followed by the outpouring of the Spirit. The blood is the life of man. The spirit is the life of God.

Ephesians 2:22

> **"In whom ye also are builded together**
> **for an habitation of God through the Spirit."**

Let us declare:

"The blood of Jesus has made me a habitation of God. I have become the temple of the Holy Spirit."

Amen

Ephesians 2:22

"In whom ye also are builded together for an habitation of God through the Spirit."

Revelation no. 22

The Blood of Jesus Christ Gives Us Access to the Promises of God

Hebrews 9:15

"And for this cause he is the mediator of the new testament, that by means of death, for the redemption of the transgressions that were under the first testament, they which are called might receive the promise of eternal inheritance."

Eternal inheritance was obtained through redemption.

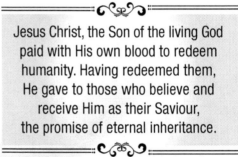

Jesus Christ, the Son of the living God paid with His own blood to redeem humanity. Having redeemed them, He gave to those who believe and receive Him as their Saviour, the promise of eternal inheritance.

The word 'eternal' not only means something that continues and has no end, but it also means it has no beginning and knows no change or decay.

The substance or life of eternity is independent of time because it is God's and He does not live in the realm of time. Everything that exists in time has a beginning and an end and is subject to the Law of increase and decrease.

The blood of Jesus has obtained
eternal inheritance that is
always glorious. Our promise
of inheritance is secure
and it will never change.

Let us declare:

"The blood of Jesus Christ has given us access to the promise of eternal inheritance."

Amen

Hebrews 9:15

"And for this cause he is the mediator of the new testament, that by means of death, for the redemption of the transgressions that were under the first testament, they which are called might receive the promise of eternal inheritance."

Revelation no. 23

Holy Spirit
Bears Witness to the
Power of the
Blood of Jesus Christ

Hebrews 9:14

> **"How much more shall the blood of Christ,
> who through the eternal Spirit offered himself
> without spot to God, purge your conscience
> from dead works to serve the living God?"**

The above scripture clearly indicates that the eternal Spirit of God waits, always ready to demonstrate to us the power that is in the blood of Jesus.

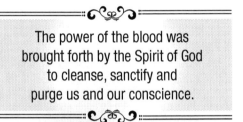

The power of the blood was
brought forth by the Spirit of God
to cleanse, sanctify and
purge us and our conscience.

Our Lord stated in *John 15:26*

> **"But when the comforter is come,
> whom I will send unto you from the Father,
> even the Spirit of truth, which proceedeth
> from the Father, he shall testify of me."**

Yes, the Comforter has arrived because of the shed blood of Christ. Think about the power of the blood of Jesus which brought God to dwell in man and man to be lifted into heavenly places.

As our Lord said, it is the work of the blessed Spirit to testify of Jesus and all that Jesus has done including His shed blood.

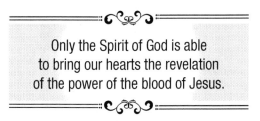

Only the Spirit of God is able
to bring our hearts the revelation
of the power of the blood of Jesus.

Let us declare:

"Lord by Your Spirit, reveal to my heart the power of the blood of Jesus so that I will walk a victorious life on earth. As You have overcome, I will also be an overcomer in You Lord. I ask and receive it in Jesus precious Name."

Amen

John 15:26

"But when the comforter is come,
whom I will send unto you
from the Father,
even the Spirit of truth,
which proceedeth from the Father,
he shall testify of me."

The Blood of Jesus Christ Cleanses the Heavens

Hebrews 9:23

> **"It was therefore necessary that the patterns of
> things in the heavens should be purified with
> these; but the heavenly things themselves with
> better sacrifices than these".**

When the word of God talks about heavens, it includes
the atmosphere, the realm where the demonic spiritual
forces operate and also the place where God dwells.

Even though we cannot see into the heavenly places
there is a tremendous amount of activity that is taking
place in this realm.

2 Corinthians 4:18

> **"While we look not at the things which are
> seen, but at the things which are not seen: for
> the things which are seen are temporal; but
> the things which are not seen are eternal."**

This clearly tells us there are two worlds, the spiritual
and the natural.

Daniel 10:13

> **"But the prince of the kingdom of Persia
> withstood me one and twenty days: but, lo,
> Michael, one of the chief princes,
> came to help me; and I remained there
> with the kings of Persia".**

The answer was delayed by twenty-one days because of the demonic activity in the heavenlies.

Thank God today we have the precious blood of Jesus which is able to cleanse the heavenlies.

> We must continue to declare
> the precious blood of Jesus
> in the heavenlies, so that
> the heavenly realm above us
> will be cleansed and sanctified
> but it will also bring
> the enemy's plans to nought.

Let us declare:

"Lord, I take the precious blood of Jesus which is able to sanctify and cleanse. I declare the blood of Jesus and cleanse and sanctify the heavenlies over my city and also the places my family and I may enter this day and night."

Amen

Hebrews 9:23

*"It was therefore necessary
that the patterns of things
in the heavens should be purified
with these; but the heavenly things
themselves with better sacrifices
than these".*

Revelation no. 25

The Blood
of Jesus Christ
Speaks for Us

Hebrews 12:24

"And to Jesus the mediator of the new covenant, and to the blood of sprinkling, that speaketh better things than that of Abel."

The word of God clearly states that the blood speaks. The writer of Hebrews wants us to know the clear distinction between the blood of Abel and the blood of Jesus Christ.

The blood of Abel and the blood of Jesus Christ speak, but the word says the blood of Jesus Christ speaks better things.

Let me give you a comparison so that you will begin to realise the importance of the blood of Jesus.

1. Abel's blood was <u>spilt</u>.
   Jesus Christ <u>shed</u> His blood.

2. Abel did not lay down his life willingly, he was murdered.
   Jesus Christ willingly gave His life; therefore He shed His blood willingly for humanity.

3. The blood of Abel was spilt on earth.
   The blood of Jesus was offered in heaven.

4. The blood of Abel speaks vengeance.
   The blood of Jesus speaks mercy.

There is a voice that continues to speak for you and me. That voice is the blood of Jesus. It cries mercy for us.

There are so many voices in the world that speak against us, but remember what the blood of Jesus speaks for you and me is greater than all the negative words.

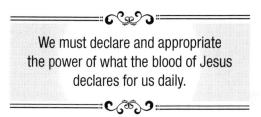

We must declare and appropriate the power of what the blood of Jesus declares for us daily.

Let us declare:

"Lord Jesus I thank You for Your blood which speaks for me and my household day and night. It speaks mercy and grace for us."

Amen

Hebrews 12:24

*"And to Jesus the mediator
of the new covenant,
and to the blood of sprinkling,
that speaketh better things
than that of Abel."*

---·⌇⌇⌇·---
Revelation no. 26
·⌇⌇⌇·---

The Blood
of Jesus Christ
is the Blood of God

Acts 20:28

**"Take heed therefore unto yourselves,
and to all the flock, over which the Holy Ghost
hath made you overseers, to feed the church of
God, for which He hath purchased with His
own blood."**

The Church belongs to God.
The church is not a denomination
or a building. The church is the body
of Christ. That is you and me.
How did we become part of the
body of Christ? Through God's blood.

Jesus Christ, the Son of the Living God is divine. He is God. God shed His own blood to purchase us.

The blood of Jesus is no ordinary blood. It is pure incorruptible blood.

Leviticus 17:11

**"For the life of the flesh is in the blood: and I
have given it to you upon the altar
to make an atonement for your souls:
for it is the blood that maketh an atonement
for the soul".**

When God shed His blood on the cross, He gave His life for you and me.

Remember you have been purchased and redeemed by God's blood. The price was paid in full for your liberty and freedom.

Let us declare:

"Thank You Father for the blood of Your Son, Jesus. The blood that redeemed me and my household is the blood of God. The blood of God is divine and holy."

Amen

Acts 20:28

*"Take heed therefore unto yourselves,
and to all the flock,
over which the Holy Ghost
hath made you overseers,
to feed the church of God,
for which He hath purchased
with His own blood."*

Revelation no. 27

The Blood
of Jesus Christ
and the Cross

Colossians 1:20

> **"And, having made peace through the blood
> of his cross, by him to reconcile all things unto
> himself by him, I say, whether they be things
> in earth, or things in heaven."**

The Apostle Paul uses the word blood of His cross. There is great significance to this statement. He was stating that it was only through the blood, the power and effectiveness of the cross was revealed.

The cross without the blood of Christ has no power or effect on any human being. It is the blood of Christ that reveals the effect and power of the finished work of the cross to every human soul.

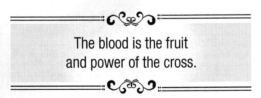

The blood is the fruit
and power of the cross.

Christ on the cross displayed to us the love of God. The blood united us to Christ and His great love.

The blood of Christ is the earthly token of the heavenly power and glory of God's love.

> The blood of Christ points us
> to the finished work of the cross
> and to the great exchange
> that took place for humanity
> on the cross of Calvary.

Let us declare:

"Lord I want to thank You that through the blood of Christ, You will reveal and impart to me and my household, the power and the effect of the finished work of the cross of Calvary."

Amen

Colossians 1:20

*"And, having made peace through
the blood of his cross,
by him to reconcile all things
unto himself by him, I say,
whether they be things in earth,
or things in heaven."*

Revelation no. 28

The Blood
of Jesus Christ
Sanctified the Altar

Exodus 29:37

"Seven days thou shalt make atonement for the altar, and sanctify it; and it shall be an altar most holy: whatsoever toucheth the altar shall be holy."

Everything that we bring to God must be holy and sanctified because he is a holy God. One of the most important articles of furniture in the tabernacle was the altar. The altar was used to present sacrifices to God.

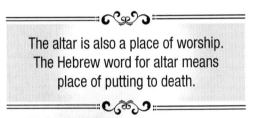

The altar is also a place of worship.
The Hebrew word for altar means
place of putting to death.

In order for God to accept the offering, not only must the offering be sanctified, but also the altar upon which the sacrifice is placed.

The blood of the sacrifice sanctified the altar, thereafter the offering was sanctified by the altar.

> Today we have the blood of
> the perfect sacrificed Lamb of God
> which is able to sanctify, not only
> the offerings that we bring to God,
> but also the heavenly
> altar forevermore.

Let us declare:

"I bring all my offerings and sacrifices unto God through the precious blood of Christ. I thank You Lord, the blood of Christ has sanctified my offering and sacrifice and now it is acceptable to God as I place them before Him through the blood."

Amen

Exodus 29:37

"Seven days thou shalt
make atonement for the altar,
and sanctify it; and it shall be
an altar most holy: whatsoever
toucheth the altar shall be holy."

---·C☙☙ᗡ·---
Revelation no. 29
---·C☙☙ᗡ·---

*The Blood
of Jesus Christ
is for
our Household*

Exodus 12:3

> **"Speak ye unto all the congregation**
> **of Israel, saying, in the tenth day of this**
> **month they shall take to them every man**
> **a lamb, according to the house**
> **of their fathers, a lamb for a house."**

In the Old Covenant, when God Almighty wanted to bring the children of Israel out of bondage, He instructed them to celebrate the Passover.

In preparation for the Passover, they had to take a lamb which would be killed during Passover. This lamb would represent the entire household.

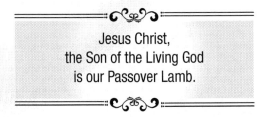

Jesus Christ,
the Son of the Living God
is our Passover Lamb.

1 Corinthians 5:7

> **"Purge out therefore the old leaven,**
> **that ye may be a new lump, as ye are**
> **unleavened. For even Christ our passover**
> **is sacrificed for us".**

> When Jesus Christ died on the cross
> and shed His blood it was not just
> for you and me, it was for
> our household. The blood of Jesus
> protects our household.

Let us declare:

"The precious blood of Jesus protects me and my household. It will keep me and my household in divine health, divine provision, and divine protection."

Amen

Exodus 12:3

"Speak ye unto all the
congregation of Israel, saying,
in the tenth day of this month
they shall take to them
every man a lamb, according
to the house of their fathers,
a lamb for a house."

Revelation no. 30

The Blood of Jesus Christ Averted the Eternal Danger

Colossians 1:13-14

**"Who hath delivered us from the power of
darkness, and hath translated us
into the kingdom of his dear Son. In whom we
have redemption through his blood,
even the forgiveness of sins."**

Sin has separated man. Sin brought a change of relationship between God with man, and also man with God.

With man, it resulted in his fall and enmity against God. With God, it resulted in His turning away from man or His wrath.

This is a terrible picture of the danger of being separated from God Almighty.

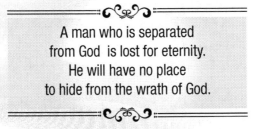

A man who is separated
from God is lost for eternity.
He will have no place
to hide from the wrath of God.

When God's Son died on the cross and shed His very blood, He brought a change of relationship between God with man and man with God. The Eternal danger was averted. Man's enmity against God was broken and God's wrath against man was removed.

Ephesians 2:16-17

> **"And that he might reconcile both unto God in one body by the cross, having slain the enmity thereby: And came and preached peace to you which were afar off, and to them that were nigh."**

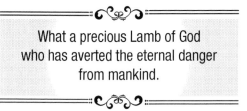

What a precious Lamb of God
who has averted the eternal danger
from mankind.

Let us declare:

"I thank You Lord for the blood of Jesus. The blood has broken all enmity that I and my household had against God and it has removed God's wrath over our lives."

Amen

Ephesians 2:16-17

"*And that he might reconcile
both unto God in one body
by the cross, having slain the enmity
thereby: And came and preached
peace to you which were afar off,
and to them that were nigh.*"

The Blood of Jesus Christ Obtains the Blessings

Exodus 12:13

"And the blood shall be to you for a token upon the houses where ye are; and when I see the blood, I will pass over you, and the plague shall not be upon you to destroy you, when I smite the land of Egypt."

The children of Israel knew when they had applied the blood on the house they were safe. God promised them that destruction would not come to their household. The word of God says, "When I see the blood, I will pass over you".

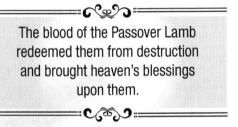

The blood of the Passover Lamb redeemed them from destruction and brought heaven's blessings upon them.

Psalms 105:37

"He brought them forth also with silver and gold and there was not one feeble person among their tribes."

How much more we, who now do not have the blood of an earthly lamb but the blood of the Lamb of God, are assured and guaranteed of the blessings of heaven.

I would like to relate this story that is recorded of an incident that may have taken place during the Passover in Egypt.

An old Israeli lived with his firstborn son. He himself was the firstborn son of his father. His son also had a firstborn son. Therefore, there were three firstborns in the same house.

Exodus 11:5

> **"And all the firstborn in the Land of Egypt shall die, from the firstborn of Pharaoh that sitteth upon his throne, even unto the firstborn of the maidservant that is behind the mill; and all the firstborn of beasts".**

The old man was sick and he was lying on his bed. He heard all that the son said to the household about God's instruction to Moses. Towards the evening of that day he became restless and began to question his son asking him, "Have you done everything correctly according to God's instruction?" The son would reply, "Yes father". For a moment he was satisfied. Again he will repeat the same question to his son. The closer it came to midnight the father became more and more restless. Finally he cried out, "Son, carry me out before midnight. I want to see the blood of the lamb on the doorpost". The son took his father and showed him. The father began to cry and thank God, "Now I can rest because I know I am safe".

Remember the blood of the
Passover Lamb of God has provided
all spiritual blessings for us.
It is our assurance and guarantee.

Let us declare:

"The blood of the Lamb of God has given me the
assurance that all God's blessings will be on me and
my household."

Amen

If you want to appropriate the blessings
of what Jesus Christ has done,
and would like to become a Christian,
then I would like you to say this prayer
with a believing heart:

Dear God in Heaven,
I come to you in the Name of Jesus.
I am sorry for my sins
and for the life I have lived.
I ask You to forgive me
and to cleanse me with Your Blood.
I believe with my heart and
confess with my mouth that
Jesus Christ is Lord.
That He died for me on the cross and
rose again on the third day.
This very moment I accept Jesus Christ
as my own personal Saviour and
according to His Word, right now I am saved.
Thank You Jesus, for dying for me and
giving me eternal life.
AMEN

Other resource material to enhance your spiritual growth and development.

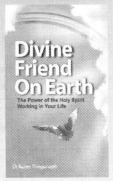

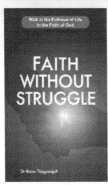

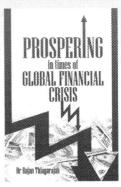

Mighty Living
Waters Life Fellowship
P O Box 183, Willetton
Western Australia 6955

email :
tv@lifeinthespirit.info

website :
www.lifeinthespirit.info

DVD

CD

Mighty Living Waters Life Fellowship
P O Box 183, Willetton
Western Australia 6955
email : tv@lifeinthespirit.info
website : www.lifeinthespirit.info